Storm Chasers

By Jim Aaron

Scott Foresman
is an imprint of

PEARSON

Glenview, Illinois • Boston, Massachusetts • Chandler, Arizona •
Upper Saddle River, New Jersey

Photographs
Every effort has been made to secure permission and provide appropriate credit for photographic material. The publisher deeply regrets any omission and pledges to correct errors called to its attention in subsequent editions.

Unless otherwise acknowledged, all photographs are the property of Pearson Education, Inc.

Photo locators denoted as follows: Top (T), Center (C), Bottom (B), Left (L), Right (R), Background (Bkgd)

Cover ©A.T. Willett/Alamy Images; **1** Chris Holland/Getty Images; **4** World Perspectives/Taxi/Getty Images; **5** (Inset) Chris Holland/Getty Images, (Bkgd) Doug Allan/Getty Images; **6** NOAA; **7** (T) David J. Phillip/©AP Images, (B) Marko Georgiev/Getty Images; **8** United States Department of the Interior; **9** NOAA; **10** NOAA; **11** Richard Cooke / Alamy Images; **12** NOAA; **13** (Inset) ©Reuters/Corbis, (T) National Hurricane Cente/AFP/Getty Images; **14** (T) NOAA, (B) Wilfredo Lee/©AP Images; **15** Jim Reed/Corbis; **16** Everett Collection, Inc.; **18** Jim West/Alamy Images; **19** Jupiter Images.

ISBN 13: 978-0-328-51648-3
ISBN 10:   0-328-51648-1

Table of Contents

Hair-raising Hurricanes

Imagine that the sun is beating down on a tropical ocean. Soon, the air begins to heat up, rise, and expand as cooler air moves in. This creates wind. If the conditions are just right, the wind will continue to get stronger until it whips the ocean waves into a frenzy. If the wind reaches 74 miles per hour, a hurricane has formed.

As more and more air is drawn into the hurricane, the winds continue to move faster and faster. Some hurricanes even have winds of several hundred miles per hour! Around the center, or "eye," of the hurricane, the winds are especially strong. Remarkably, at the center of the hurricane in the eye, the weather is calm and still.

Hurricane clouds swirl at top speed around a calm center, or "eye."

A hurricane forms above the sea.

On land, hurricanes cause major destruction.

Many hurricanes stay out in the ocean. However, if a hurricane reaches land, watch out! These storms can be extremely dangerous. Their winds can damage or even destroy houses, telephone poles, cars, and roads. People who don't get out of the path of a hurricane can be blown off their feet, injured, or even killed by objects flying through the air.

As a result of heavy rain and rising seas, hurricanes often cause flooding. Near the eye of a hurricane, where the air **pressure** is low, the sea can rise as much as 12 feet above normal. That situation can cause massive floods.

How are storms measured? Storms are measured using different **scales**. The Saffir-Simpson Hurricane Scale is used throughout the world. It rates hurricanes from Category 1 to Category 5. A Category 1 indicates the weakest and least harmful hurricanes. A Category 5 indicates the strongest and most destructive ones.

In August 2005, a hurricane named Katrina formed over the Atlantic Ocean near the Bahamas. As it traveled toward the Gulf Coast of the United States, the storm grew stronger. In time, it became a Category 3 hurricane and one of the most destructive hurricanes in history. Approximately 1,800 people are thought to have died because of it. The cost of Hurricane Katrina is still being calculated. However, it is thought to have caused more than 200 billion dollars in damage.

Saffir/Simpson Hurricane Scale

Category	Definition
ONE	Winds 74-95 mph
TWO	Winds 96-110 mph
THREE	Winds 111-130 mph
FOUR	Winds 131-155 mph
FIVE	Winds greater than 155 mph

The Saffir-Simpson Hurricane Scale is used to measure the force of hurricanes.

Hurricane Katrina devastated New Orleans and much of the surrounding Gulf Coast.

One of the most startling things about Hurricane Katrina was the way it affected the Gulf Coast. At the time of the storm, the water was up to 20 feet deep in some areas. In fact, parts of the coastline were simply washed away.

Thousands of people lost their homes as a result of the storm. Many still do not have a permanent place to live. All of this has been especially hard on the children of the Gulf Coast. Many of them missed school for months after the disaster, and many are still suffering.

Compare these photographs of the Chandeleur Islands, before and after Hurricane Katrina.

July 17, 2001

August 31, 2005

A tornado's dark color is caused by the debris and dirt it picks up.

Terrible Twisters

A tornado is similar to a hurricane in that it is a kind of funnel of air that swirls around, causing a destructive wind. It is formed at the base of a thundercloud over flat land. As warm, wet air rises up through colder air at the bottom of a cloud, Earth's rotation makes the air spin and form a funnel. The low air pressure inside this funnel acts like a vacuum. Its winds can spin more than 300 miles per hour, picking up anything in its path. Each year in the United States, tornadoes kill about 70 people and injure around another 1,500.

Each year in an area of the United States called "Tornado Alley," hundreds of tornadoes occur. They tend to appear in the summer when the warm air from the Gulf of Mexico meets cold air coming down from Canada, causing thunderstorms.

Tornadoes can vary tremendously. One tornado can last just a minute, whereas another can last for an hour. Additionally, some tornadoes can be very weak, and others can be very violent.

A map of Tornado Alley

Tornadoes are known to do surprising things. For instance, in an area where there might only be a thunder and lightning storm, it can suddenly start raining frogs and fishes! When a tornado passes over water, it can lift small animals into the air. It then carries them for a distance, but when the tornado loses its power, it will drop the animals down wherever it happens to be at the moment.

Another strange event happened in 1915 when a tornado completely destroyed a farm. Even from close up, you would never have known an entire farm had been there! The only evidence of its existence were five horses that were found a quarter of a mile away. They were completely unharmed and still tied to the same fence rail!

Tornadoes, as well as hurricanes, can have long-lasting and very serious effects. For instance, damage to water-processing plants can lead to the **chemical** contamination of drinking water. Life in towns and cities can be affected if farms, **manufacturing** plants, and other businesses are destroyed or damaged.

Tornadoes have been known to cause strange events such as animals falling from the sky.

Many scientists believe that global warming can cause more frequent and severe storms. The National Aeronautics and Space Administration (NASA) believes that the warming of Earth's **atmosphere** creates many more extremely high clouds. High clouds can cause especially severe storms and excessive rainfall. However, not all experts agree. In 2005 several meteorologists wrote an **essay** saying that there was not enough evidence to make such claims.

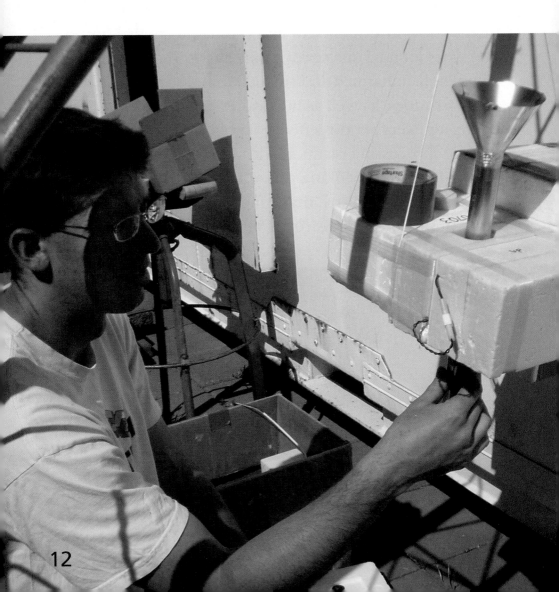

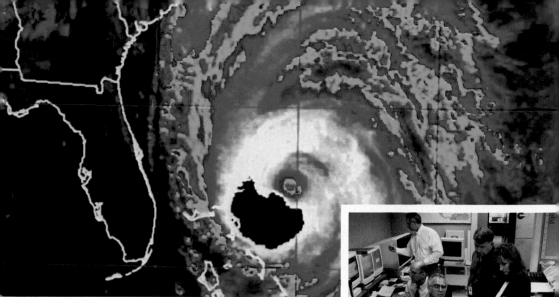

Doppler radar imaging helps scientists track hurricanes.

The Storm Chasers

How do we know so much about hurricanes and tornadoes? Throughout history, these intense storms have fascinated people who have observed them with the naked eye, as well as with scientific instruments. In 1935 the National Hurricane Center was established near

The National Hurricane Center on the campus of Florida International University

Miami, Florida. The low, flat, concrete building was constructed to withstand forceful winds and floods. Scientists there gather information that helps to save lives and protect property from hurricanes.

How do scientists study hurricanes? They use a variety of equipment, including maps, computers, satellite tracking, and hurricane-hunting planes. They also actually fly into storms.

13

Can you imagine flying into the eye of a hurricane? That is the risky job of the highly skilled pilots who fly planes called hurricane hunters directly into storms. Scientists also ride along, using special onboard equipment to gather information about a hurricane. Today the National Oceanic and Atmospheric Administration (NOAA), a government agency, oversees the National Hurricane Center and many of the hurricane hunters.

Hurricane-hunting planes flew through the eye of Hurricane Katrina.

These storm chasers are monitoring a severe storm.

Meteorologist Chris Landsea of the National Hurricane Center described flying into the eye of a storm. He said that "sunshine streams into the windows of the plane from a perfect circle of blue sky. Around the edges of this calm circle, dark, angry thunderclouds threaten, and far below the ocean rages."

In the future, "drones," or remote-controlled planes, may take over most hurricane-hunting missions in order to lessen the danger for the scientists who study them.

In recent years, scientists are no longer the only ones chasing hurricanes and tornadoes. Ordinary people may **apprentice** themselves to professional storm chasers or form a **club** to explore their interest with others. Why do they do it? There is the thrill of being caught in a raging storm. There is also the satisfaction of taking amazing photographs or video footage. But make no mistake about it: storm chasing is extremely dangerous.

The movie *Twister* helped make storm chasing popular.

Movies and television shows have helped fuel interest in storm chasing. One movie told the story of two groups of scientists competing with each other to chase and study an enormous tornado. Many people felt that this movie did not portray tornadoes, or tornado chasing, correctly. They said there were many scenes in which the storms in real life would have killed people but those people didn't die in the film. Also, they said the storm was shown blowing objects out rather than sucking them in, as tornados actually do.

Storm Safety

Is it possible to stay safe in a hurricane or tornado? Yes, but it does take some planning and preparation.

You can learn to detect an approaching storm simply by looking outside. Dark or strange-colored clouds, hail, and a loud, roaring sound can all indicate an approaching tornado. Weather reports on the radio or television also help alert people that a hurricane or tornado is on the way.

When people know they will be living in an area where tornadoes occur more frequently, the first thing they should do is determine a safe shelter. People living in a mobile home should find a stronger building in which to weather a tornado or hurricane. In a tornado, stay away from windows, which may shatter. Knowing these things ahead of time will allow the person to react quickly and wisely when they see the strange clouds approaching.

The American Red Cross is an organization that helps people affected by natural disasters. It is one of the best emergency response organizations. The Red Cross provides information about how to get ready and be prepared for storms. When storms hit, the American Red Cross is often on the scene, providing temporary shelter, food, blankets, and other supplies. From the time they were formed as an organization more than one hundred years ago, they have helped millions of people survive and recover from natural disasters.

An American Red Cross shelter during Hurricane Ivan in 2004

Scientists will continue to study hurricanes and tornadoes to understand what causes them and how best to predict them. The more they research, the more information can be gathered. And with that new information, the better people can be protected from violent and dangerous storms. While one day we hope to be able to predict the formation and movements of hurricanes and tornadoes, as of today we cannot. Therefore, simply being prepared is the best way to be safe during a storm.

Glossary

apprentice *v.* the act of learning a trade or art by working for an expert

atmosphere *n.* the mass of gases surrounding the earth; the air

chemical *adj.* having to do with or used in chemistry; any substance used in a chemical process

club *n.* a group of people joined together for a special purpose

essay *n.* a paper or composition written on a specific subject

manufacturing *v.* making by hand or machine, usually in large quantities

pressure *n.* the continued action of a weight or force

scales *n.* instruments used for weighing or measuring things